PragerU

PragerU is redefining how people think about media and education. Watched millions of times every day, PragerU is the world's leading nonprofit with educational, entertaining, pro-American videos for every age. From intellectual, fact-based 5-Minute Videos and powerful personal storytelling to animated shows made just for kids—PragerU helps people of all ages think and live better.

PragerU Kids teaches history, civics, financial literacy, and American values to children across the K-12th grade spectrum. With kids shows, books, and educational resources for every grade, PragerU Kids offers content that parents and teachers trust and children love. Watch for free and learn more at PragerUkids.com.

Published by PragerU

15021 Ventura Boulevard #552

Sherman Oaks, CA 91403

Presidents
of the
United States of America

Table of Contents

Dwight D. Eisenhower

"I helped the Allies win World War II and served as the 34th President of the United States."

AMERICA'S 34th PRESIDENT

Become a Presidential Historian by Solving This Puzzle

In this book, you'll learn all sorts of facts about Dwight D. Eisenhower's amazing life and accomplishments. But there's still one last thing we need to know about him.

President Eisenhower had a dog as a pet. We need your help to find out what her name was. Your task is to help us uncover the answer! Hidden in the text are bolded letters. Read this book carefully to find them, and fill the letters into the blanks below in the order they appear.

— — — — —

Once you've solved this puzzle, you'll be a true PragerU Kids presidential historian!

Meet Dwight D. Eisenhower

The **Cold War** was a scary time. America had a dangerous enemy–**communism**–and there was always the fear that war could break out at any moment. Even worse, both sides had fearsome **nuclear weapons** that could destroy all of humanity. In the 1950s, the American people wanted someone with experience and wisdom to lead them through this terrifying period. Thankfully, they had someone perfect for the job: the heroic general of **World War II**, Dwight D. Eisenhower.

During that war, Eisenhower led America to victory against the **fascist** government of **Nazi Germany**. He had organized Operation Overlord–the largest seaborne invasion in world history. He had demonstrated great leadership skills–abilities that Americans wanted in a president.

While Eisenhower rose to fame in wartime, as president, he worked hard to keep America at peace. He masterfully managed several crises during his time in the White House. He helped to keep the Cold War from breaking out into a hot war, and he helped ensure that America remained the technological leader of the world. Many Americans celebrate his presidency as a time of peace and prosperity.

Young Ike

Dwight David Eisenhower was born on October 14, 1890, in Denison, Texas. He was the third of David and Ida Eisenhower's seven children—all boys. His parents initially named him David Dwight Eisenhower, but when this caused confusion (his father was also named David), they began calling him by his middle name, Dwight. They also gave him the nickname "Little Ike."

Ike's father, David, was a mechanic, and their family had little money. Young Ike, however, was an active boy: when he wasn't doing chores, he was hunting, fishing, and playing football.

After graduating high school in 1909, Ike was admitted to the **United States Military Academy** at West Point, New York. He was an average student and, upon graduation, was commissioned a Second Lieutenant.

Interesting Facts

- He is the last general (as of 2024) to serve as president.

- He was a member of the Republican Party.

- He signed a law in 1956 officially declaring "In God We Trust" as the nation's motto.

- He was the first president to preside over all 50 states (with the addition of Alaska and Hawaii to the Union in 1959).

- He was the first president to travel by jet aircraft.

- He was the first president to appear on colored television.

- He was the first president to win an Emmy Award.

- In his youth, he loved playing football and baseball. He was also a master poker player. In his later years, he relaxed by playing golf.

- He has been honored on the one-dollar coin and with a national memorial in Washington, D.C.

Upper: Young Ike and his brothers
Lower: Young Ike with his high school football team

3

Early Career

Life in the military took Eisenhower from station to station across the country. While at Fort Sam Houston in San Antonio, Texas, he met a young woman named Mamie Doud. They fell in love and married in 1916. He and Mamie eventually had two sons, Doud and John. Tragically, Doud died of scarlet fever in 1921 at the age of three.

When America entered World War I in 1917, Eisenhower wanted to be close to the action in Europe like many of his fellow soldiers. He was disappointed, however, when he was assigned to stay in the United States training tank crews.

After the war, Eisenhower worked as an aide to several top Army leaders: Fox Conner, John J. Pershing, Douglas MacArthur, and George C. Marshall. He also studied at the Command and General Staff College at Fort Leavenworth, Kansas. Unlike at West Point, Eisenhower did very well and even graduated first in his class in 1926 out of 245 officers. During this time, Eisenhower mastered military history and strategy by reading classic works, such as Carl von Clausewitz's *On War*. This knowledge would serve him and the country well in the future.

While serving under General MacArthur in the 1930s, Eisenhower was stationed in the Philippines, where he helped train the Filipino army. By this time, he had attained the rank of colonel.

Quote

"The proudest human that walks the earth is a free American citizen."
- May 1948

World War II

After World War II broke out in Europe in 1939, President Franklin D. Roosevelt began preparing America for the possibility of entering the war. Eisenhower did his part by leading training exercises in Louisiana. He impressed Army leaders with his talent for planning and strategy and was promoted to brigadier general.

After America entered the war in 1941, Eisenhower worked for Army Chief of Staff George C. Marshall as a war planner. He won General Marshall's trust and was given several important assignments, such as planning the invasions of North Africa, Sicily, and Italy.

Eisenhower's successes caught the eye of President Roosevelt. The president promoted him as Supreme Commander of the Allied Expeditionary Forces in Europe. He even chose Eisenhower for the most important assignment of them all: Operation Overlord, also known as D-Day.

D-Day

Since 1939, the Nazi government, under German dictator Adolf Hitler, had taken over much of Europe, destroying cities and murdering millions of people. The Soviet Union, led by communist dictator Joseph Stalin, was stuck doing most of the fighting against the Nazis. Stalin knew, however, that the Nazis couldn't be defeated unless the Americans joined in. By 1944, the United States was ready to take the Nazis head-on.

Eisenhower, now a four-star general, organized the critical invasion, which would take place on the beaches of Normandy, France. He knew how big this responsibility was and cared deeply about the men he was sending to battle. Just before the invasion, named **D-Day**, he spoke to the soldiers and said, "You are about to embark upon the Great Crusade, toward which we have striven these many months. The eyes of the world are upon you. The hopes and prayers of liberty-loving people everywhere march with you."

On June 6, 1944, the largest invasion in human history commenced, combining land, air, and sea forces from America, Britain, and Canada. One hundred fifty-six thousand troops—supported by almost 7,000 vessels and 11,000 aircraft—began an all-out assault on Hitler's forces in France.

The invasion was very complicated and had to be carefully planned by Eisenhower. He had even faked a potential invasion of another region in France, Pas-de-Calais, to throw the Nazis off. Eisenhower had a speech prepared in case the invasion failed, in which he would take full responsibility.

Thankfully, he never had to give that speech. Despite the fierce German onslaught, the Allies triumphed, and Hitler's grip on Europe began to crumble. By the time the Nazis surrendered in May 1945, General Eisenhower was a **five-star general** and an international hero.

5

The 1952 Presidential Election

After the war, Eisenhower wrote his memoir, *Crusade in Europe.* His heroics from World War II made him an instant presidential candidate.

As a military man, Eisenhower had not identified with any political party, but in early 1952, he announced that he was a Republican. At the time, many Republicans wanted America to be less involved with world affairs and focus on itself. These people were often called **isolationists**. Unfortunately, the communists, led by America's former ally, the Soviet Union, were aggressively expanding around the world and taking away freedom from their populations, imprisoning, and even killing, millions of people. Eisenhower believed that America, with all of its strength, couldn't be isolationist—it had an important role to play in keeping the peace and stopping the Soviets. He ran for president for this reason.

The Republicans nominated him for president and the young senator from California, Richard Nixon, for vice president. The Eisenhower campaign ran with the catchy slogan, "I Like Ike." That fall, they defeated the Democratic ticket of Adlai Stevenson and John Sparkman in a landslide, 442 electoral votes to 89.

Quote

"History does not long entrust the care of freedom to the weak or the timid."
- January 1953

President

Dwight Eisenhower took office in the midst of the Cold War—a conflict between the United States and the Soviet Union (and its ally, communist China). It was a terrifying time, especially since both sides had nuclear weapons which could destroy all of humanity. During Eisenhower's presidency, America and the communists had several dangerous confrontations in places like Taiwan, Hungary, and the Middle East that easily could have led to nuclear war. The leader of the Soviet Union, Nikita Khrushchev, was an unpredictable man who loved to bully other countries.

Eisenhower refused to be intimidated and often responded with strength. During several of these confrontations, he threatened to stop the communists with military action, which forced the enemy to back down. He also negotiated to end the **Korean War**, which paved the way for a decade of peace and prosperity in the United States.

Eisenhower also presided over the rise of the civil rights movement in the United States. In 1954, the Supreme Court declared that racial segregation was unconstitutional. When many Southerners tried to maintain segregation, Eisenhower sent the military in to enforce the Court's decision.

The American people loved Eisenhower and re-elected him to the presidency by a wide margin in 1956.

Eisenhower also signed several laws to modernize the country and prepare it for the complexities of the future. He established the **Interstate Highway System**, which led to the building of about 46,000 miles of highway. He also created the **Advanced Research Projects Agency** (ARPA) and the **National Aeronautics and Space Administration** (NASA). Although some criticized him because they felt these projects were too expensive, he believed they would ensure America's leadership in technology and space exploration.

Even though the Cold War was a dangerous situation, Eisenhower successfully led America through eight years of peace. He left the presidency an admired and popular figure.

Quote

"A people that values its privileges above its principles soon loses both."
- January 1953

Presidents of the United States of America: Dwight D. Eisenhower

Farewell Address

Just before leaving office, on January 17, 1961, Eisenhower delivered his farewell address to the American people—the most famous presidential farewell message since George Washington's in 1796. In it, he insisted that the country needed a strong defense: "Our [military] arms must be mighty… so that no potential aggressor may be tempted to risk his own destruction." However, he warned Americans to make sure that the nation didn't become too militaristic, or else it would become less free. He reminded them to keep an eye on the "**military-industrial complex**… so that security and liberty may prosper together." To this day, Americans still debate how much power should be given to the military while also preserving the nation's liberty.

Retirement

Eisenhower and his wife Mamie retired to a farm in Gettysburg, Pennsylvania. By then, he was 70 years old—the oldest outgoing president. By contrast, his successor, John F. Kennedy, at age 43, was the youngest president ever elected.

Eisenhower remained active in retirement, writing books and giving advice to subsequent presidents, including Kennedy and Lyndon B. Johnson. In 1968, he had the pleasure of seeing his former vice president, Richard Nixon, elected president. By then, his health was failing, having suffered through several heart attacks. He died of heart failure on March 28, 1969, in Washington, D.C. at the age of 78.

Writing Activity

President Eisenhower organized D-Day, as well as many projects throughout his career. Write about what you can learn about his leadership and organization.

Quote

"Faith is the mightiest force that man has at his command. It impels human beings to greatness in thought and word and deed."
- August 1954

Legacy

Eisenhower was one of the most popular presidents in American history. Many professors and media commentators, however, claimed that he was lazy and ill-equipped to be the nation's chief executive. The more historians studied him over the years, however, the more they realized that his critics were wrong. Everyone who worked with Eisenhower knew he was a highly intelligent and capable leader. How else was he able to successfully organize history's greatest invasion? In addition, Eisenhower laid the foundation for America to eventually win the Cold War. Thanks to his foresight, planning, and preparations, the United States had the technology to compete with the Soviet Union for the next several decades.

After Eisenhower left office, the nation went through very difficult times under his successors Kennedy, Johnson, and Nixon. Throughout the 1960s and 70s, the American people suffered through the Vietnam War and the Watergate Scandal. When they looked back at Eisenhower, they had a greater appreciation of how he kept the country peaceful and prosperous. Now, Americans, and even many professors, consider Eisenhower to be one of the nation's most effective presidents.

Sources

Gaddis, John Lewis. *Strategies of Containment: A Critical Appraisal of Postwar American National Security.* Oxford University Press, 1982.

Newton, Jim. *Eisenhower: The White House Years.* Doubleday, 2011.

Pach, Chester J. "Dwight D. Eisenhower." *Miller Center, University of Virginia,* https://millercenter.org/president/eisenhower/. Accessed 31 January 2023.

Reeves, Thomas C. "Dwight D. Eisenhower." *Encyclopedia Britannica,* https://www.britannica.com/biography/Dwight-D-Eisenhower/. Accessed 31 January 2023.

"The Eisenhowers: Dwight David Eisenhower Chronology." *Dwight D. Eisenhower Presidential Library, Museum & Boyhood Home,* https://www.eisenhowerlibrary.gov/eisenhowers/. Accessed 31 January 2023.

Thomas, Evan. *Ike's Bluff: President Eisenhower's Secret Battle to Save the World.* Little, Brown and Company, 2012.

Images: Getty Images, WikiCommons, FreePix

Answers

NAME OF EISENHOWER'S DOG:
HEIDI

Glossary

Cold War: The conflict between America, which was free, and the Soviet Union, which was a communist dictatorship, that lasted from the 1940s to the late 1980s.

Communism: A political and economic system where all property and resources are owned and controlled by the government. The result of this system is often dictatorship and government control of every aspect of people's lives.

Nuclear Weapon: A weapon that uses a nuclear reaction to create a massive explosion, which can destroy a large area, such as a city. When it was developed in the 1940s, it was the most powerful weapon ever created.

World War II: A war that involved many of the world's countries from 1939 to 1945. During the war, the Allied powers, led by the United States, the United Kingdom, and the Soviet Union, defeated the Axis powers, led by Nazi Germany, Italy, and Japan. It is considered the most devastating war in history.

Fascist: A dangerous and oppressive type of government where one person has all the power and makes all the decisions. It promotes extreme loyalty to the homeland and often believes one ethnic group is better than others. Individual rights and freedoms are not respected, and people are not allowed to criticize the leader or government.

Nazi Germany: The German state from 1933 to 1945 when it was ruled by Adolf Hitler. Nazi Germany was a totalitarian dictatorship that aggressively invaded its neighbors, provoking World War II. It also committed evil acts of genocide—most famously killing millions of Jews in the Holocaust.

United States Military Academy: The U.S. Army's top military academy, which provides undergraduate education and training to commissioned Army officers. It is known as West Point and is located in New York State. Dwight Eisenhower graduated from West Point in 1915.

D-Day: The codeword for the Allied invasion of Normandy, France on June 6, 1944. It was the largest seaborne invasion in history and was organized by General Dwight D. Eisenhower. The success of the invasion led to the liberation of France and, ultimately, the defeat of Nazi Germany.

Five-Star General: The highest military rank in the United States Army. Dwight D. Eisenhower was one of nine Americans (as of 2024) to have attained the rank of a five-star officer.

Isolationist: Someone who believes their country should avoid getting involved in the affairs of other nations and focus on its own issues and interests, preferring to keep their country separated from international conflicts and interactions.

Korean War: A military conflict from 1950 until 1953 that began when communists in North Korea, supported by China and the Soviet Union, tried to impose a dictatorship over the entire country. The United States sent about 6.8 million soldiers to support the South Koreans, preventing the communists from taking over the entire Korean Peninsula.

Interstate Highway System: The network of highways built across the United States to make travel safer and more efficient. President Eisenhower signed the system into law in 1956, which led to the building of 46,000 miles of highway. Eisenhower also believed that the highways would allow for a stronger national defense.

Advanced Research Projects Agency: The U.S. government agency (now known as the Defense Advanced Research Projects Agency, or DARPA) that develops new technologies for the military. DARPA has been responsible for developing weather satellites, GPS, drones, stealth technology, the personal computer, and the Internet.

National Aeronautics and Space Administration: The U.S. government agency, known as NASA, responsible for space exploration. It has achieved spectacular successes with its manned space program, especially during the Apollo moon missions and the Space Shuttle.

Military-Industrial Complex: The relationship between the U.S. military, the defense industry, and politicians. While most Americans believe in the need for a strong military, many fear that this relationship often leads to costly programs that help companies and politicians without improving the nation's defense.

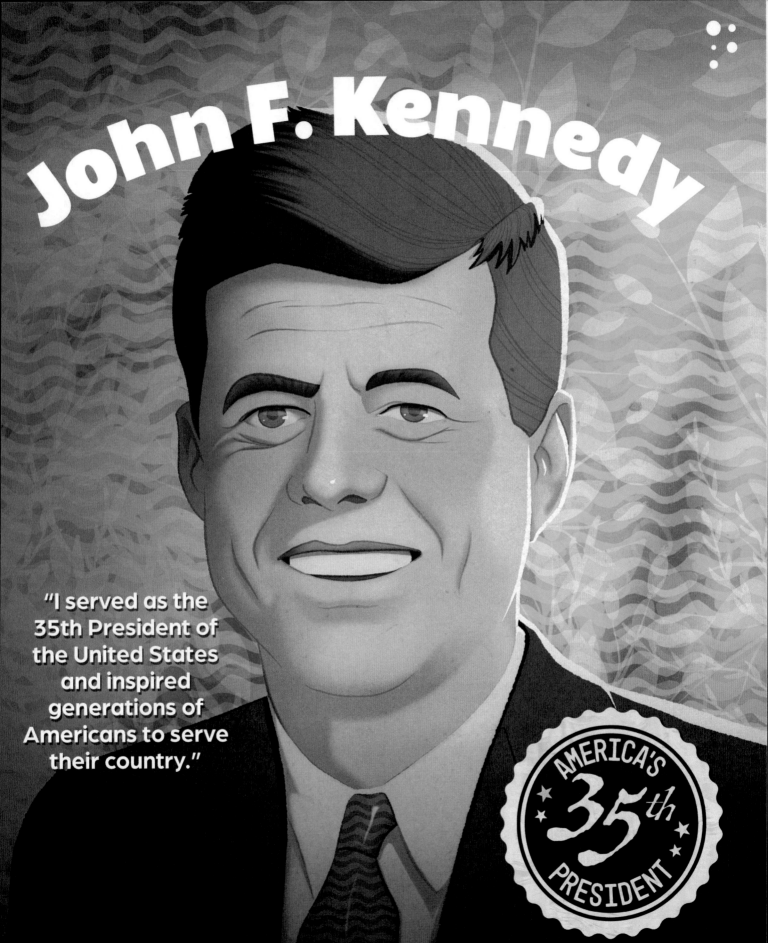

Become a Presidential Historian by Solving This Puzzle

In this book, you'll learn all sorts of facts about John F. Kennedy's amazing life and accomplishments. But there's still one last thing we need to know about him.

His daughter Caroline had a pet pony. We need your help to find out what its name was. Your task is to help us uncover the answer! Hidden in the text are bolded letters. Read this book carefully to find them, and fill in the letters in the blanks below in the order they appear.

— — — — — — — — —

Once you've solved this puzzle, you'll be a true PragerU Kids presidential historian!

Meet John F. Kennedy

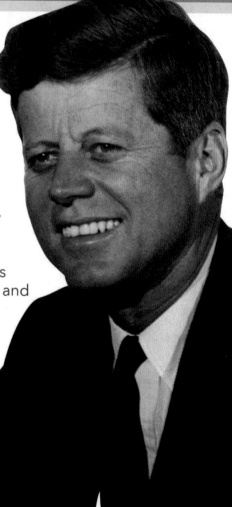

Have you ever felt inspired by someone before? That's how John F. Kennedy made Americans feel. He gave speeches that motivated people to do their best. He constantly challenged them to serve their country and achieve great things.

Americans loved him for many other reasons too. He was young, handsome, and intelligent. They adored his beautiful wife and their young children. They loved having such a youthful and vibrant family in the White House.

It all came to a tragic end on November 22, 1963, when Kennedy was assassinated in Dallas, Texas. People around the world were stunned and saddened by his death. They couldn't believe that someone with so much promise could be taken away so suddenly.

Ever since his death, Americans have learned more about Kennedy. They learned that he had many secrets in his private life—that he wasn't always honest with the American people. Also, he wasn't always successful in everything he did as president.

Despite these new insights, Kennedy remains one of the most popular presidents in history. His words continue to inspire new generations of Americans.

Young Jack

John Fitzgerald Kennedy was born on May 29, 1917, in Brookline, **M**assachusetts. He was nicknamed "Jack" and was the second of Joseph and Rose Kennedy's nine children. The Irish-**Roman Catholic** Kennedys were loyal Democrats and one of the most prominent families in Boston.

Jack's father, Joseph, was a successful businessman. He was very ambitious and would eventually serve in important positions under President Franklin D. Roosevelt. He instilled in his children a strong sense of competition and **a**n interest in sports and politics.

Joseph had exceptionally high hopes for his oldest child, Joseph Jr., grooming him to become the first Catholic president. By contrast, little was expected from Jack. Unlike Joe Jr., Jack was an average student and was often sick. He spent much time in bed suffering from various illnesses: bronchitis, chicken pox, measles, mumps, scarlet fever, and whooping cough. He later developed severe back problems that would plague him for the rest of his life.

Still, Jack and his family lived a privileged life. They traveled to Hyannis Port on Cape Cod in the summers, where they spent their days swimming, sailing, and playing touch football.

Jack and his siblings went to the best schools. In 1936, he enrolled in Harvard University, where he studied politics and **c**ompeted on the swim team. Jack loved learning about international affairs and even wrote a long essay about the situation in Europe just before World War II, titled "Appeasement in Munich." It eventually became a bestselling book under the title *Why England Slept*.

13

Interesting Facts

- He was, at 43 years old, the youngest man ever elected president (as of 2024).

- He was a member of the Democratic Party.

- He was nicknamed "Jack" and is often called "JFK."

- He was the first president to be born in the 20th century.

- He was the first Roman Catholic to serve as president.

- He was the first president who had previously served in the U.S. Navy.

- He is (as of 2024) the only president to have won the Pulitzer Prize for the book *Profiles In Courage*.

- He was the fourth president to be assassinated.

- He is (as of 2024) the president with the shortest lifespan—46 years.

- NASA's Kennedy Space Center, the Kennedy Center in Washington, D.C., and John F. Kennedy International Airport in New York are all named after him. In addition, his face appears on the half-dollar.

World War II

In 1941, one year after Kennedy graduated from Harvard, the United States entered **World War II**. He joined the Navy and, thanks to his father's connections, got an assignment as the commander of a **patrol torpedo (PT) boat** in the South Pacific. His boat was designated PT-109.

It was a dangerous job; in fact, in August 1943, his boat was rammed and destroyed by a Japanese destroyer. Kennedy led his crew as they swam for hours through the fiery wreckage of their boat and toward the nearest island. He even towed a badly injured crewmember with him by clenching the man's life jacket straps in his teeth. After arriving on the island, they were eventually rescued by another PT boat.

Kennedy was awarded the **Navy and Marine Corps Medal** and the **Purple Heart Medal** for saving his crew. The family was proud of him for his courage. Unfortunately, soon after, the Kennedys suffered a devastating loss: in August of 1944, Joe Jr., who was serving as a bomber pilot in Europe, died in a tragic accident. Jack was crushed, but he had no time to be sad. Now, his father's hopes for Joe Jr. to become president were transferred onto Jack.

Jack on a PT boat

Jack and Joe Jr. in uniform

Rise to Power

In 1946, Kennedy was elected to Congress as a Democratic representative from Boston. He was just 29 years old and an up-and-coming politician. The Kennedys suffered another tragedy, however, when his beloved sister Kathleen died in a plane crash in 1948.

Despite this terrible loss, Kennedy continued to have great ambitions. In 1952, he won a seat as a senator from Massachusetts. During that year, his younger brother Robert, or "Bobby," managed his successful campaign. The two brothers became very close, and eventually, Bobby became his most trusted advisor.

By then, Kennedy had met a beautiful young woman named Jacqueline Lee Bouvier, or "Jackie." She also came from a prominent and wealthy family. They married in September 1953 and eventually had three children: Caroline, John Jr. (nicknamed "John-John"), and Patrick. Tragedy struck once again when Patrick died in infancy.

The Cold War

During Kennedy's time in the Senate, America was in the middle of the **Cold War**—a dangerous time when the nation faced the threat of **communism**. Wherever the communists took power, freedom disappeared, and millions were executed or tossed into prison.

America's main enemy was the Soviet Union, the world's most powerful communist country. At the same time, the United States and the Soviet Union had **nuclear weapons** capable of destroying the world. Many people feared that if both sides went to war, civilization itself would end.

Kennedy strongly opposed communism and believed America was the world's only hope for freedom. In 1952, he stated that the communists were "an enemy… unrelenting and impeccable who seeks to dominate the world."

Although the president at the time, Dwight D. Eisenhower, also opposed communism, Kennedy felt he could do a better job stopping the Soviets.

The 1960 Presidential Election

Kennedy was very popular in Massachusetts and won re-election by a wide margin in 1958. This time, his youngest brother Edward, or "Teddy," managed his campaign. JFK was now being discussed as a possible presidential candidate. Since he was still very young—in his early 40s—many people felt he should wait a few years and get more experience.

Kennedy rejected this advice. He felt life was about taking chances, so he announced he was running for the presidency in 1960. He performed well in the primary elections against his opponents, Minnesota Senator Hubert Humphrey and Texas Senator Lyndon B. Johnson. At the Democratic Convention in July, he easily won the nomination.

He also chose Senator Johnson as his running mate. Many people felt that Kennedy—a senator from New

England—chose Johnson, a Southerner, because he needed support from the South to win the election.

Kennedy faced the Republican candidate Richard Nixon, the sitting vice president, in the general election. Although Nixon had more experience in a higher office, JFK had a way with words and inspired the American people with his speeches. He argued that the United States was failing to defend freedom and that he would "get the country moving again." Kennedy called his program the "New Frontier" and promised that he could boldly lead the country into the 1960s.

Kennedy and Nixon faced off in the first televised presidential **debates** in American history. It was the first time voters could see the two candidates discuss the major issues face-to-face. Most presidential elections since have featured these debates, but Kennedy and Nixon started this tradition.

In November of 1960, Kennedy won the election by a narrow margin—49.7% to 49.5% in the popular vote. At 43, he was the youngest man ever elected to the presidency.

KENNEDY FOR PRESIDENT

LEADERSHIP FOR THE 60's

Quote

"I believe in an America that is on the march—an America respected by all nations, friends and foes alike... a strong America in a world of peace."
- October 1960

President

On January 20, 1961, Kennedy took the oath of office to become America's 35th president. He then delivered one of the most famous speeches in the nation's history, in which he challenged Americans to,

> "Ask not what your country can do for you—ask what you can do for your country."

Kennedy's presidency was a tumultuous time for the United States. Although he had promised to counter the Soviets, he launched a failed invasion of Cuba–known as the **Bay of Pigs Invasion**. It was a major embarrassment. The Soviets believed JFK was weak and felt they could bully him by secretly sending nuclear missiles to Cuba. These missiles made many American cities vulnerable to nuclear attack.

When Kennedy discovered the missiles in October 1962, he demanded that Soviet leader Nikita Khrushchev remove them. Khrushchev refused at first. The situation, now known as the **Cuban Missile Crisis**, became very tense, and everyone feared nuclear war would break out. Some say it was the closest that the world came to being destroyed. Kennedy held firm, and Khrushchev eventually gave in to his demand. The Soviets removed the missiles, and the crisis ended.

JFK also tried to stop the communists as they took over the Southeast Asian nation of Vietnam. He sent over thousands of military officials to Vietnam and feared that if the communists took over that country, they would spread across all of Southeast Asia.

Finally, Kennedy presided over the growing **civil rights movement** led by Dr. Martin Luther King Jr. In 1963, Kennedy proposed a civil rights bill to end segregation and protect the voting rights of all Americans regardless of their race.

Quote

"An economy hampered by restrictive tax rates will never produce enough revenues to balance our budget—just as it will never produce enough jobs or enough profits."
- December 1962

17

The Space Race

During the Cold War, the United States and the Soviet Union competed in many ways—economically and militarily. Both sides strove to be the world leader in as many arenas as possible. The most exciting arena at the time was space. The Soviets had beaten America in October 1957 by putting the first satellite, Sputnik, into orbit. They then beat America again in April 1961 by putting the first man, Yuri Gagarin, in space. The American people feared that if the Soviets kept winning the **space race**, the world would believe communism was the superior system.

Kennedy had had enough. In May 1961, he announced that America had a new goal: to put a man on the moon by 1970. He believed that, while the Soviets were ahead for the time being, Americans had the genius to beat them to the moon in the long run. Although many people felt JFK's vision was too ambitious, he was proven right when Apollo 11 astronauts Neil Armstrong and Edwin "Buzz" Aldrin landed on the moon in July 1969.

Quote

"We choose to go to the moon in this decade and do the other things, not because they are easy, but because they are hard."
- September 1962

Assassination

By the fall of 1963, Kennedy began planning for his 1964 re-election campaign. He knew he needed to strengthen his support in the South to win again, so he traveled with his wife Jackie to Texas to meet with important officials and give speeches. On the afternoon of Friday, November 22, 1963, he and Jackie were riding in an automobile through the streets of Dallas, waving to the crowd, when shots suddenly rang out. One of those shots struck Kennedy in the head, killing him.

The nation was shocked. Although his presidency had been tumultuous, JFK and his family were very popular. Americans couldn't believe that such a young, charismatic leader could be taken from them in such a violent way. From then on, millions of people around the world would remember exactly where they were and what they were doing when they heard about the assassination.

A few hours after the shooting, the police arrested a 24-year-old man named Lee Harvey Oswald and announced that he was suspected of killing Kennedy. Two days later, as he was being transferred to a nearby jail, a man named Jack Ruby shot and killed Oswald. The shooting had taken place on national television. Americans were traumatized by Kennedy's assassination and shocked by Oswald's murder.

Quote

"The cost of freedom is always high, but Americans have always paid it. And one path we shall never choose... is the path of surrender or submission."
- October 1962

A Widow's Grief and a Son's Salute

On November 25, 1963, Kennedy's funeral took place in Washington, D.C. His widow Jackie and his brothers, Bobby and Teddy, walked solemnly through the streets of the capital behind his coffin. People around the world were touched that Jackie Kennedy had the strength to appear in public at the funeral, despite witnessing the horror of her husband's assassination just days earlier.

In a tragic coincidence, Kennedy's son, John-John, had turned three that exact day. Millions of Americans would never forget seeing little John-John salute his father's casket on the saddest of all possible birthdays.

Conspiracy?

Oswald's death meant he would never be tried in a court of law. This left many questions unanswered. To answer these questions, the new president, Lyndon B. Johnson, established a group called the Warren Commission to investigate the assassination. The Commission's report, released in September 1964, declared that Lee Harvey Oswald had killed JFK alone. The fact that Oswald was killed, however, has convinced many Americans that there was a bigger conspiracy at work and that someone wanted Oswald killed so that he wouldn't reveal the true story. People have made a lot of money writing books and producing movies and documentaries supporting these **conspiracy theories.**

Others, however, believe that the evidence supports the Warren Commission's conclusion. They point to Oswald's own personal history—he was an abusive husband, a violent man, and a strong supporter of communism—that makes him the likely assassin. They also point out evidence they believe implicates Oswald, such as the fact that his palm print was on the rifle used to kill Kennedy. In fact, Oswald's own brother Robert believed that he was guilty.

The debate over who killed Kennedy continues to this day.

American Royalty

The Kennedys, along with the Adamses, the Roosevelts, the Tafts, and the Bushes, are among America's most successful political families. Even though the United States does not have a monarchy, many consider them the equivalent of the nation's royal family. Millions of Americans have admired their youth, glamor, and charisma.

Both of Kennedy's grandfathers were prominent Boston politicians. His father, Joseph Sr., was a top official in President Franklin D. Roosevelt's administration. During JFK's presidency, his brother Bobby was a member of his Cabinet (as Attorney General) and his closest advisor, while his other brother Teddy served in the U.S. Senate. Bobby eventually became a senator, and both he and Teddy ran for president themselves.

The Kennedy family's involvement in politics continued into the next generation. JFK's daughter Caroline has served as a diplomat, and his son John Jr. was a prominent attorney and magazine executive. His nephews and nieces have also had prominent careers in politics and media.

While the Kennedys have enjoyed great success, they have also experienced great tragedy. Kennedy, his siblings Joe Jr., Kathleen, Bobby, and his son John Jr. all suffered violent deaths at relatively young ages. His other sister Rosemary became severely mentally disabled after a botched surgery. Bobby ran for president in 1968 but was assassinated as well. All of these tragedies have led some to believe that the Kennedy family is cursed.

Controversies

The Kennedy family has also been very controversial. Many historians and writers have presented evidence that they were corrupt and often misbehaved in their private lives. For instance, Teddy was involved in a car accident in 1969 in which a young woman died, but a judge gave him lenient punishment. Some believe this punishment was unfair and that Teddy got off easy because of his family's power and influence.

Critics also point out that the family has kept many secrets about their private lives. For example, the family kept many of JFK's health issues hidden from the public eye. Some say the American people should have known about their president's health issues because they could have affected his performance.

Legacy

Despite these controversies, John F. Kennedy remains one of the most popular American presidents of all time. To this day, his speeches and life story continue to inspire people around the world. He seemed to have it all: good looks, money, power, and intelligence. These qualities made him an admired figure for millions around the world.

When someone inspires so much hope in others, they may have difficulty living up to expectations. As president, Kennedy promised to "get the country moving again" against the Soviets and defend freedom. This looked like an empty promise when he launched a foolish and poorly-planned invasion of Cuba.

Kennedy is often praised for acting decisively during the Cuban Missile Crisis: he was able to force the Soviets to remove the missiles while also preventing nuclear war from breaking out. At the same time, many believe that had he not botched the Bay of Pigs Invasion, the Soviets wouldn't have sensed weakness and put missiles in Cuba in the first place.

While Kennedy might not have lived up to all expectations, he strongly believed in American freedom and ingenuity. Ever since his assassination, millions of Americans have yearned for a leader who could inspire them once again.

Quote

"The rights of man come not from the generosity of the state but from the hand of God."
- January 1961

Writing Activity

The Space Race was a battle of intelligence rather than physical strength. Do your own research about the first man on the moon and write about what you've learned.

Sources

Brinkley, Alan. *John F. Kennedy: The American Presidents Series: The 35th President, 1961-1963*. Times Books, 2012.

Dallek, Robert. *John F. Kennedy: An Unfinished Life, 1917 - 1963*. Penguin Books, 2003.

Gaddis, John Lewis. *Strategies of Containment: A Critical Appraisal of Postwar American National Security*. Oxford University Press, 1982.

Giglio, James N. *The Presidency of John F. Kennedy*. University Press of Kansas, 2006.

"Life of John F. Kennedy." *John F. Kennedy Presidential Library and Museum,* https://www.jfklibrary.org/learn/about- jfk/life-of-john-f-kennedy/. Accessed 1 January 2023.

Reeves, Richard. *President Kennedy: Profile of Power*. Simon & Schuster, 1993.

Selverstone, Mark J. "John F. Kennedy." *Miller Center, University of Virginia,* https://millercenter.org/president/kennedy/. Accessed 1 February 2023.

Answers

NAME OF KENNEDY'S DAUGHTER'S PET PONY:
MACARONI

Glossary

Roman Catholic: A branch of Christianity that follows the teachings and traditions of the Catholic Church, led by the Pope in Rome. Roman Catholicism is one of the largest religions in the world, with over 1 billion followers.

World War II: A war that involved many of the world's countries from 1939 to 1945. During the war, the Allied powers, led by the United States, the United Kingdom, and the Soviet Union, defeated the Axis powers, led by Nazi Germany, Italy, and Japan. It is considered the most devastating war in history.

Patrol Torpedo (PT) Boat: A small, fast naval vessel used for patrolling, scouting, and launching torpedo attacks by the U.S. Navy in World War II, Korea, and Vietnam. It was armed with underwater weapons called torpedoes and was used to attack enemy vessels and shore installations and support and rescue friendly troops and pilots.

Navy and Marine Corps Medal: An award given to members of the United States Navy and Marine Corps who show bravery and heroism while risking their own lives to save others.

Purple Heart Medal: An award given to military members who were injured or killed while serving the United States of America in combat.

Cold War: The conflict between America, which was free, and the Soviet Union, which was a communist dictatorship, that lasted from the 1940s to the late 1980s.

Communism: A political and economic system where all property and resources are owned and controlled by the government. The result of this system is often dictatorship and government control of every aspect of people's lives.

Nuclear Weapon: A weapon that uses a nuclear reaction to create a massive explosion, which can destroy a large area, such as a city. When it was developed in the 1940s, it was the most powerful weapon ever created.

Debate: A public discussion of important issues between candidates for political office.

Bay of Pigs Invasion: A failed American invasion of the island of Cuba in April 1961. President Kennedy approved the invasion, which was planned by the Central Intelligence Agency, to remove Fidel Castro's communist government from power. The failure of the invasion convinced the Soviets that Kennedy was weak and encouraged them to send nuclear missiles to Cuba.

Cuban Missile Crisis: A major confrontation between the United States and the Soviet Union in October 1962. The Soviets secretly shipped several nuclear missiles to Cuba to threaten cities in the United States. President Kennedy demanded that the missiles be removed. Initially, the Soviets refused to remove the missiles, and the world feared that a nuclear war might erupt. Kennedy remained firm, and, after a couple of tense weeks, the Soviets removed the missiles, and the crisis ended. Some believe that the crisis was the closest the world came to nuclear war.

Civil Rights Movement: A struggle throughout the 1950s and 1960s to secure equal rights and opportunities for black Americans. The movement sought to challenge and eliminate racial segregation, discrimination, and racism in the United States. The movement, led by prominent figures such as Dr. Martin Luther King Jr., utilized non-violent protests to achieve racial equality before the law.

Space Race: A competition between the United States and the Soviet Union during the 1950s and 1960s to determine which nation was the worldwide leader in space exploration. Initially, the Soviet Union leaped ahead in the race by placing the first satellite and the first man in space. In 1961, President Kennedy set a new goal: to land a man on the moon by 1970. NASA achieved this goal in July 1969 when Apollo 11 astronauts Neil Armstrong and Edwin "Buzz" Aldrin became the first men to walk on the moon.

Conspiracy Theory: A belief that an event or a set of circumstances is the result of a secret plot by powerful people.

Notes

READY FOR MORE?

Experience all the **FREE CONTENT**
PragerU Kids has to offer!

STREAM FREE SHOWS ON YOUR TV OR TABLET

Download our FREE mobile or TV app to stream every PragerU Kids show! Or, watch any time at PragerUkids.com.

ENJOY HOURS OF FREE SHOWS

Browse over 300 educational videos for K-12, including game shows, cartoons, and inspiring reality shows.

EXPLORE WHOLESOME STORIES & AMAZING HISTORY

Download free e-books at PragerUkids.com or purchase printed copies on Amazon.

FREE RESOURCES FOR TEACHERS & PARENTS

Supplement your child's viewing experience with lesson plans & worksheets that meet educational standards.

Experience Fun, Interactive, and Educational Content at
PRAGERUKIDS.COM